Original title:
The Reef's Silent Witness

Copyright © 2025 Creative Arts Management OÜ
All rights reserved.

Author: Harris Montgomery
ISBN HARDBACK: 978-1-80587-446-1
ISBN PAPERBACK: 978-1-80587-916-9

Lament of the Anemone

In the shallows, I sway and dance,
With fish that tickle, but not romance.
Jellyfish glide, oh what a sight,
Yet they forget to turn off the light!

Oh, the coral fights over sunbeam space,
While sea cucumbers just lounge with grace.
We're all just waiting for the tide's call,
But I swear that clownfish eats too much—after all!

Silent Observers of Solitude

In the depths, we watch the fun,
A hermit crab races, look at him run!
A floaty jelly takes a wrong turn,
While octopus plots—oh, how we learn!

Sea urchins gossip, spines at the ready,
Claiming the reef's both lush and heady.
Starfish play cards, dealing with flair,
But wave after wave, it's hard to keep fair!

Timeless Tales of the Tide

Every wave tells a story untold,
Like fish that claim treasures of old.
Crabs with their pinchers try to impress,
While seahorses wear ties—a bit of a mess!

Clownfish and tangs in dramatic debate,
Who stole the seaweed? Someone's late!
Anemones giggle, with tentacles twirl,
As bubbles float by in a watery swirl!

Murmurs from the Sea Floor

On the seabed, we share our dreams,
With sand dollars smiling, or so it seems.
A pufferfish quips, 'I've got more air!'
While snails leave trails, claiming it's fair.

Cuttlefish plotting some great escapade,
Laughing at mergansers, they just can't evade.
In this underwater realm of delight,
Let's all enjoy the next ocean fight!

The Guardian in Tidal Hues

In shades of blue, a fish got stuck,
A seaweed hat, oh what bad luck!
He swam around with a grumpy frown,
Wishing for more than this green gown.

A crab passed by with a cheeky grin,
"Hey, buddy, just go with the fin!"
The fish replied with a bubble of spite,
"At least you don't have to wear this kite!"

Silent Echoes of Aquatic Life

A clam once held a gossip spree,
Said, "Did you see the octopus, oh me!"
With eight tiny arms, he danced a jig,
While the sea anemone laughed, so big!

From the deep, a whale made a call,
"I'm more graceful, friends, look at my sprawl!"
But the squid replied with a winking glance,
"Sure, you're big, but do the waltz dance!"

Beneath the Layers of Seafoam

A fish in the foam tried to play hide-and-seek,
But his bright colors made him rather weak!
Too easy to spot in the soft, gentle tide,
With a puff of sea air, oh how he cried!

A dolphin laughed, flipping high in the air,
"Come on, my friend, let down your hair!"
So they all joined in a splashy charade,
Pretending to be in a grand mermaid parade!

Stories Carried by Currents

A sea turtle rolled, living the dream,
"I'm the king of this wave, or so it would seem!"
But each little bump on his shell made him squeak,
"These currents aren't turning, they're feeling quite weak!"

A school of fish tried to tell him a tale,
"It's not hard, just follow the trail!"
But he just chuckled and swam on ahead,
"With so many stories, I'll dance instead!"

Midnight Whispers of the Sea

A crab in a tux, so dapper and neat,
Climbs high on his rock, such a sight to greet.
Fish gossip in schools, in shimmering schools,
While dolphins do dive, breaking all the rules.

A clam with a secret, it pouts with a frown,
Wonders why oysters wear pearls like a crown.
Seahorses tango, in swirling ballet,
They giggle and twirl, 'Oh, what a display!'

Heralds of the Hidden Depths

A snail with a flair, cartwheels on the sand,
While jellyfish float by, oh, isn't life grand?
Anemones sway, waving hello to the day,
While octopuses ponder, 'What game shall we play?'

A parrotfish sings, tuneless yet so bold,
Says, 'Watch out, dear pals, for that seaweed so old!'
The humor of tide pools, with snickers and quirks,
Bubbles burst laughter, as nature just smirks.

Secrets Silently Conveyed

In the dark of the night, a starfish turns glum,
While barnacles jest, 'Hey, where's your fun?'
Coral reefs bend, like they're laughing at lies,
As turtles do somersaults, wise before wise.

A flatfish, so sneaky, hides in plain sight,
Whispers of sea-brush, in moonbeams so bright.
The giggling petrels squeak, like a novel delight,
As waves wince with tickles, in frothy moonlight.

Murmurs in the Water's Embrace

An old eel tells tales, with a wink of his eye,
To the fishes who gather and wiggle nearby.
Nudibranchs flaunt colors, a vibrant parade,
While seagulls cackle jokes that never quite fade.

A flounder finds wisdom hiding in mud,
Claims, 'Life's a big splash, or a small little thud!'
The whispers of bubbles float gently around,
As laughter and joy in the ocean abound.

Shadows of the Underwater Realm

In the depths where fish gossip,
Coral castles sway like dancers,
Anemones pull funny faces,
While sea turtles wear their stances.

Starfish play peek-a-boo games,
Shrimp snap jokes on the soft sand,
Crabs do the cha-cha with flair,
In this underwater wonderland.

Mussels whisper like old friends,
Seahorses giggle as they pass,
Jellyfish float in a soft trance,
Laughing at the currents' sass.

The octopus writes a memoir,
In ink that blots with great style,
Every creature keeps a secret,
In this aquatic comic mile.

The Watcher Adrift

A pufferfish looks on puzzled,
Does he puff up for a hug?
The clownfish, full of laughter,
Is dressed up like a snug bug.

Seahorses strut in slow motion,
Bragging about their sunken car,
A dolphin makes a big splash,
While nearby, a starfish plays guitar.

In the kelp, the seaweed sways,
Making faces at passing rays,
While crabs scuttle with a prance,
Joining the delightful dance.

The watcher adrift can't help smile,
As chaos reigns in ocean blue,
For in this realm of silly fish,
Even waves seem to laugh too.

Symphony of Sheltered Lives

Clams clap with rocky applause,
Harmonies bubble under the tide,
Fish tickle the ocean floor,
While laughter rises like a ride.

Surfers of the sea grass bend,
Blowfish blow, a balloon parade,
Crab races with the tide so fast,
In the folly where jokes are made.

Oysters keep their secrets tight,
Laughing softly behind their shells,
While rays dance up above,
To the ocean's giddy bells.

The symphony's madcap sounds,
Bring joy to the sea's own heart,
In this world beneath the waves,
Where silliness is an art.

Tales of the Submerged Realm

Once a fish lost his own tail,
Sought it out from the bottom's maze,
Found it wrapped around a rock,
And they both had a laugh for days.

Turtles tell of races won,
With tales that grow taller each time,
As jellyfish float through the scene,
Spreading stories as light as rhyme.

An octopus juggles with flair,
Tentacles swirling in mid-air,
While eels pretend to be snakes,
In a playful underwater dare.

Each creature here knows a jest,
Fin to fin, they share a grin,
For in these waters so alive,
The fun never seems to thin.

The Inaudible Keeper

In the deep where fish do dance,
A crab once gave a sideways glance.
With whispers soft as sea foam's breath,
He guards the tales of love and death.

A seahorse laughed at a turtle's plight,
While octopuses stayed up all night.
The anemones giggled at passing ships,
As waves tickled their vibrant tips.

A dolphin dove and made a jest,
Of squids who claim they're the best.
But secrets float, they dare not sway,
For in silence, their stories stay.

So, next time you're down by the shore,
Listen closely, there's so much more.
An underwater comedy quite divine,
With laughs and quirks on every line.

The Ocean's Gentle Witness

Below the waves, a clam, quite sly,
Watches fish like a sharp-eyed guy.
With pearls of wisdom hidden tight,
He chuckles softly at their plight.

A starfish gave a wink and grin,
To all the crabs who think they win.
They scuttle fast; they really try,
While seaweed sways and rolls its eye.

Mollusks gossip, calling names,
About those fish and their silly games.
"Oh look, there goes a clownfish now,
Wearing stripes but can't take a bow!"

As bubbles rise, the laughter spreads,
A silly tale beneath our beds.
For in the deep, where stories lie,
The ocean's humor will catch your eye.

Currents of Unseen Stories

In the depths, the tides do play,
Dancing fish in a grand ballet.
An urchin chuckles, a quiet chap,
While jellyfish float with a gentle flap.

Whispers glide on currents swift,
Of a grouper who gave a gift.
It turned out to be a soggy sock,
Oh, the laughter, they'll never mock!

A school of minnows lost their way,
And stumbled into an old mermaid's bay.
With tales of pirates and treasures bright,
They giggled through the starry night.

So, next time you hear the ocean sigh,
Remember the laughter that slips by.
For hidden songs and tales abound,
In every wave, a joy is found.

Expressions of the Abyss

Down in the dark, where shadows lurk,
A minnow plotted a little quirk.
He'd dress as a shark, alarm all the schools,
But the joke fell flat; who knew fish have rules?

An eel wrapped up in a silly dance,
Made everyone stop and take a chance.
With twists and flips, he swirled around,
While other fish laughed, a joyful sound.

Coral sings in colors bright,
While shy fish hide, avoiding the light.
Every bubble is a giggle shared,
In this watery world, all stories aired.

So dive beneath, let your heart rejoice,
In the depths where sea creatures have a voice.
For every ripple carries a tale,
Of a world under, where humor prevails.

Silence In the Seascape

Bubbles float by, making a show,
Fish wear masks, an underwater glow.
Crabs dance sideways, thinking they're slick,
While seaweed laughs, with a slapstick flick.

A dolphin giggles, spinning in glee,
And octopuses juggle, just wait and see!
Starfish take selfies, a beach day delight,
Under the waves, everything feels right.

Coral tells tales of time long gone,
In a language as sweet as an ocean's song.
The sea cucumbers start a debate,
On who wears the best shade of seaweed plate.

Seahorses fashion a trendy new line,
While turtles play poker, sipping fine brine.
In this watery world, laughter is rife,
As creatures spin stories; it's a splash of life.

The Calm of Subaquatic Vigilance

Way down deep where the sunlight fades,
Fish gossip daily, swapping charades.
Anemones tickle, oh what a sight,
While clowns play tricks, just for delight.

A grouper's grumpy; he lost a bet,
To a sneaky shrimp that he can't forget.
The eels in their den hide smiles so sly,
As jellyfish float with a wink of an eye.

Anglerfish grins with a lightbulb above,
Prepping for dinner, looking for love.
The pufferfish puffs, and what a display,
He's the life of the party; it's all in play.

In a world of wonders, laughter rings clear,
Even in depths where we shed a tear.
Each flick of a fin carries joy and cheer,
In this vibrant ocean, no room for fear.

Twilight of the Coral Guardians

As dusk settles in, the fish start to dance,
With skeletons of coral in a trance.
Shells clink like glasses in a rave of glee,
While sea stars groan, 'Oh, let us be free!'

Crustaceans flip burgers on a hot rock grill,
As narwhals join in, loving the thrill.
The reef's party rolls on through the night,
With moonlit waves casting silver light.

A hermit crab struts in a borrowed shell,
Thinking he's trendy, but who can tell?
The clownfish chuckle, spinning their tales,
While the ocean hums soft, like faint old gales.

Coral guardians laugh, keeping watch with pride,
Of fishy frolics and secrets they hide.
In this vast playground of blue and of green,
The ocean's own jesters reign supreme.

Echoes of Submerged Tranquility

In the sea, fish flit and glide,
One wears a hat, oh what a ride!
A turtle sneezes with a loud honk,
While crabs play cards on a seaweed wonk.

Underwater, laughter bubbles rise,
A starfish winks with a big surprise!
The dolphins chuckle, sharing a joke,
While sea cucumbers just sit and poke.

In coral castles, the clams all dance,
A seahorse prances in a funny stance!
They toss around a shiny shell,
And giggle together, oh how they swell!

Bubbles rise up, as they all convene,
With fishy puns, their world is a scene!
In this watery realm, joy's quite the treat,
Where laughter lingers, and life is sweet.

Hidden Eyes of the Deep

Beneath the waves, a fish gives chase,
Wearing a tie, at a stylish pace!
An octopus hides, playing peek-a-boo,
With ink-splat humor, it's quite the view!

Crabs hold a feast, with seaweed as menus,
The snails sip soup, dreaming of venues,
A jellyfish floats, all grace and flair,
While sea urchins giggle, spiking the air!

Tangled nets make a game of fun,
A snapper shouts, "Let's play, everyone!"
The hidden eyes peek out in delight,
And the ocean winks, deep into the night.

In corners of blue, the laughter expands,
With bubbles of joy floating through their hands!
Where the oddest fish still try to glide,
It's a quirky world, their secret guide.

Voices in the Aquarium

In the glass tank, the crowd's alive,
With witty quips, the fish all jive!
A goldfish grins, colors so bright,
Swapping tales of their nightly flight.

The angelfish squabble, a lively debate,
"Who steals the worms? Oh, just wait!"
A little guppy blushes, turns a shade green,
In this bustling school, laughter's the scene!

A clownfish juggles some shimmering shells,
While loopy seaweed weaves all the spells.
They share warm stories of coral and tides,
United in giggles where joy abides.

Chirps and bubbles rise through the dare,
As the shy shrimps inch closer to share!
With announcements and glee from where they reside,
These underwater critters joyfully glide.

Secrets of the Undersea

Under the waves, mischief's abound,
A pufferfish puffs, spinning around!
With gossip and giggles, they fluster and flirt,
As sea turtles dance in their brand new shirt.

Clownfish crack jokes, bright orange delight,
While crabs in the sand dance into the night!
Shrimps share the news of a glorious feast,
While the shy octopus dreams up a beast.

With shells used as drums, the tunes come alive,
A conch plays a rhythm, oh what a vibe!
Sea stars clap along with their five-pointed hands,
As fish celebrate their little blunders and plans.

In caverns and crevices, secrets are spun,
Where laughter and bubbles unite as one!
With underwater humor, they splash and play,
In a world where the sun and silly fish sway.

Shadows in the Brine

Beneath the waves, where laughter hides,
A crab wearing glasses, he's full of pride.
Fish joke around, in their finny dance,
The seaweed sways in a greenish trance.

A seahorse winks, quite sly and spry,
"Join our conga, without a sigh!"
Starfish giggle, they're having a ball,
"Who's got the snacks? We'll share them all!"

Octopus plays cards with a clever twist,
"Pull a fast one? Now, who'd have guessed?"
Jellyfish float in a dazzling swirl,
"Dance on my tentacles, give it a twirl!"

So dive on in, bring your silly hat,
Join the undersea party; imagine that!
In the depths of the brine, laughter does thrive,
Where bubbles and giggles keep us alive.

Memories of Ocean's Embrace

Once upon a bubble, a fish wore a tie,
"Sophisticated gills, look at me fly!"
The dolphins chuckled, surfed in a line,
"Buddy, relax, you're looking just fine!"

A turtle on a skateboard zooms past a reef,
"Watch out for that wave; it's a big leap!"
The clownfish snicker, playing tricks profound,
"Can you catch us, slowpoke? We'll see who's crowned!"

With shells for trumpets, they play a fine tune,
"We'll serenade the starry sea moon!"
In coral caverns, a giggle parade,
"Why so serious? Come join the charade!"

So let's make memories, splash in delight,
Under the sun, where sea sparkles bright.
In this watery world, let fun be your chase,
Where laughter and joy come woven in grace.

Sentinel of the Blue Depths

An old fish with wisdom, gray and grand,
Tells tales of adventure, as he darts through sand.
"Once I caught a wave, and I flew like a kite,
But tripped on a clam, oh what a sight!"

A dolphin with pearls, prances with glee,
"I once held a party for jellyfish, whee!"
With bubbles for drinks and seaweed for cake,
They danced till dawn, what a splash they'd make!

A wise octopus, in her clever disguise,
Claims she's an artist, displaying her pies.
"Who wants a tasting? It's certainly grand!
Just ignore the taste; my presentation's the brand!"

So come heed the stories of this salty brigade,
Where giggles emerge in the depths of the shade.
Under the waves, our silliness flows,
In the laughter of currents, joy only grows.

Watcher of Colorful Shores

On a pebbled beach, where seashells lay,
A crab in a bow tie is leading the play.
"Who's ready for relay? I'll be the judge!
Just don't drop the seashells; it's really a grudge!"

The starfish wave banners, all bright and bold,
"Join our race; it's a sight to behold!
But first, a quick foot rub, for our prickly selves,
Then we'll race each other, let's put on our shelves!"

Seagulls are swooping, in comedic flair,
"Yo ho, me hearties! Can you fly in the air?"
Belly flops erupt, from bold fish on land,
"Oops! I forgot that I'm not so well-planned!"

So dance on the shore, and giggle with glee,
For life at the beach is a humorous spree.
The waves break with laughter, the sun's shining bright,
Under the sky, everything feels just right.

Tides of Untold Stories

Beneath the waves where secrets lie,
A fish tells tales, with a wink and a sigh.
The starfish giggles, all snug on a stone,
As crabs tap dance, they're never alone.

A seahorse prances, all decked in flair,
While turtles debate who has the best hair.
The ocean's a stage, with laughter in tow,
As jellyfish shimmy, putting on a show.

Whispers of Underwater Love

Two clams in a shell, they snuggle so tight,
While grouper take selfies, oh what a sight!
Anemones blush, waving their threads,
While pufferfish giggle, puffing their heads.

Star-crossed shrimp dance, a love that's so bold,
With garland of seaweed, their tale is retold.
In the depth of the ocean, where romance takes flight,
Even the crabs trade their claws for the night!

Guardians of Coral Beauty

Coral towers rise, dressed in bright hues,
While fish in tuxedos turn heads, they can't lose.
A clownfish tells jokes, with a laugh and a spit,
While angelfish gossip, can't handle their wit.

The sea turtles watch, in their wise old way,
As octopuses juggle, both night and day.
In the kingdom of colors, they rule with great glee,
These guardians of beauty, forever carefree.

Heartbeats of Hidden Waters

In shadows and currents, the sea critters dwell,
With hearts made of bubbles, they know how to swell.
A dolphin who raps, with a flow full of cheer,
While minnows all join in, lending an ear.

The seaweed sways gently, a dance that's so fine,
As flounders go flat, saying, 'Is this my line?'
With laughter that echoes, and joy that won't cease,
The heartbeats of waters bring humor and peace.

The Monitors of Marine Harmony

Amid the bubbles, fish hold court,
With coral crowns, they strut and sport.
The sea's full of giggles, it's clear as day,
As crabs dance a jig in watery ballet.

An octopus juggles shells with flair,
While starfish wonder, 'Is this a fair share?'
The shrimp form a band, all ready to play,
In this underwater cabaret, bright and gay.

The sea cucumbers chuckle in glee,
As clownfish crack jokes beneath the sea.
The currents hum tunes that tickle and tease,
Making waves of laughter ripple with ease.

So beneath the blue, with giggles abound,
The underwater world spins round and round.
Silent witnesses of fun down below,
Where laughter and bubbles eternally flow.

Graceful Watchers of the Abyss

In the deep blue, a turtle glides,
Spying on shrimp in their hide-and-seek rides.
With a wink and a wave, it steals the show,
While sea anemones dance to and fro.

Seahorses prance in a wavy line,
In their underwater ball, they sip on brine.
With tiny top hats and a twirl, they say,
'We're the fanciest folks of the ocean café!'

Giant clams boast pearls that gleam and shine,
While fish weave gossip through kelp intertwine.
Anemones chuckle as they catch some rays,
Watching the antics of their swimming frays.

Beneath the sunbeams, joy is a must,
Where laughter flows deeper than ancient crust.
Graceful watchers of silliness glide,
In the vastness where laughter can't hide.

Symphony of Silent Depths

In darkened waters, a party begins,
As jellyfish twirl in their glowing spins.
Each bob and weave, a note in the song,
Creating a melody where all fish belong.

The clowns in the sea tell tales of yore,
While hermit crabs sneak across the ocean floor.
With a flip and a flop, an eel hums a tune,
As sea urchins chuckle under the moon.

A whale's distant song brings giggles galore,
While dolphins leap high, seeking an encore.
The ocean's orchestra plays a fine set,
Making waves of laughter you'll never forget.

In silent depths where joy takes its flight,
The music of life makes everything bright.
In an underwater symphony, so grand,
The creatures keep time with a comical hand.

Life's Unheard Narration

In sleepy lagoons where mischief thrives,
A pufferfish whispers, 'It's time to surprise!'
With bulging cheeks and quite the flair,
It tells the tales of adventures rare.

The little clownfish play peekaboo,
In the seaweed jungles, they wave at you.
With each playful dart, they weave a sly plot,
Where laughter erupts, it's nearly too hot.

Starfish lounge like experts of leisure,
Debating the best method to measure.
While barnacles mumble with crusty old grace,
Tales of their travels in this aquatic space.

So down in the depths where stories are spun,
Life's unheard narration is constant fun.
With every splash, every bubble, we write,
The joyous saga of depth's sheer delight.

The Aquatic Guardian

A fish in shades of blue and green,
Hiding secrets, quite unseen.
With a smile and a wink so sly,
He keeps watch as the sea creatures fly.

Crabs scuttle, looking quite absurd,
While turtles ponder, oh so blurred.
An octopus juggles pearls with glee,
In this world where all are free.

Coral reefs burst with colors bright,
While jellyfish dance, it's quite a sight.
But the fish just yawns and kicks up sand,
Guarding the tale of the ocean's grand.

When you think he's just lazy and calm,
He's crafting tales that could charm.
For under the surface, laughter stirs,
In the watery depths, everyone purrs!

Beneath Surface Stillness

Bubbles rise like laughs in the air,
Clownfish giggle without a care.
With seaweed wigs, they dance and sway,
On this strange underwater stage play.

Anemones wave like flags of cheer,
While seahorses whisper, 'Come near!'
They gossip about crabs with their clumsy ways,
Critiquing their moves for endless days.

Starfish ponder deep philosophical thoughts,
While shrimps plot dances, in mischief they're caught.
With every tide, new jokes arise,
Hidden laughter beneath sapphire skies!

In this kingdom, the fish do jest,
Life's a comic show, they've made it the best.
So dive on down, join this witty spree,
For nothing goes deeper than fishy glee!

Unvoiced Tales of the Tides

Along the waves, where whispers collide,
Fish flip jokes like a rollicking ride.
They share secrets in voices unclear,
Bubbling laughter will draw you near.

Each shell holds a story, each nook a laugh,
As dolphins plot their next big gaffe.
With flippers crossed, they dream of pranks,
While stingrays glide through balancing ranks.

The sea floor's a carpet of coral delight,
Stars of the ocean, glowing so bright.
But hidden within their charming glows,
Lie tales of flubs, where mischief flows.

Come closer, dear friend, hear the unvoiced,
Join the tide where laughter's rejoiced.
Every splash tells a joke, every swirl an art,
In a world of wonder, we'll play our part!

Silenced Legends of the Deep

In waters dark, where shadows creep,
The fish conspire, their promises deep.
With scales that shimmer, a sneaky lot,
They share giggles when no one's caught.

A walrus holds court with a wobbly grin,
Telling tales of jellyfish's silly spin.
The clownfish snorts; they turn, they roll,
While sea cucumbers just play the role.

In caves where silence brings out the weird,
There's laughter aplenty, but wisdom's smeared.
For every rock or cave or sweep,
There lies a legend that tickles the deep.

So take a dive, join the crew,
Where every wave is something new.
In this salty playground of privileged belief,
The fun of the ocean is our shared relief!

Whispers Beneath the Waves

Fish gossip freely, it's quite a sight,
Octopus blushing, oh what a fright!
Sea turtles chuckle, blowing bubbles wide,
Clownfish giggle, on a joyride.

Anemones sway, dancing in the light,
Hermit crabs wear their homes, oh what a plight!
Starfish laugh at the clueless nautilus,
Underwater shenanigans, ready to fuss!

Jellyfish jiggle, with their squishy flair,
Seahorses strut, in their vibrant wear.
Lobsters grumble, snapping their claws,
In this silly world, everyone guffaws!

Bubbles rise high, like balloons in the air,
Under the sun, no worries or care.
The ocean's a party, where laughter's the game,
Remember, in water, it's never the same!

Guardians of the Ocean Floor

Crabs in uniform, patrolling the sand,
With tiny helmets, they make a grand stand.
Mollusks sports coats, so suave and sleek,
Gossiping kelp, oh what a cheek!

Eels in tuxedos, all dressed up to play,
Throwing underwater parties all day.
Flounders flip-flop, pulling off their disguise,
While penguins waddle with mischievous eyes.

A pufferfish poses, puffed up with pride,
While clownfish laugh, and their secrets confide.
A whale in a top hat, how dapper and grand,
Singing sea shanties, join in the band!

Oysters clapping, pearls fall like rain,
Acquiring a talent, in all this refrain.
The ocean, a theatre, where fun is the core,
Guardians of laughter, forever we adore!

Echoes of the Coral Kingdom

Coral castles, in colors so bright,
Hold secrets of giggles, in the soft twilight.
Anglers dangle hooks, all tricked out with glee,
While parrotfish chuckle, 'Come swim with me!'

Seashells echo, tales from the deep,
Sardines shimmy, in schools they leap.
The sea cucumbers, wise in their way,
Share nuggets of humor, night and day.

Barnacles mingle, always in style,
Comically crusty, with laughter and guile.
A dolphin cracks jokes, on a watery spree,
Every wave carries whispers, just wait and see!

Bubbles of laughter, rising with grace,
In the coral kingdom, joy finds its place.
The ocean's a party, where silliness swells,
In a world that's enchanted, where laughter compels!

Dreams in Aquatic Shadows

In shadows beneath, where sea creatures play,
Blennies tell tales of their funny foray.
Squid scribble stories in ink clouds so grand,
While lanternfish twinkle, like stars they stand.

Waves whisper secrets to the playful fry,
Sea otters giggle, as they chase and pry.
A grouper's retelling, an epic tall tale,
Of adventures he had, where he's never so pale!

The night brings a chorus of chuckles and sighs,
With glowing ideas that light up the skies.
The ocean's a dreamscape, where laughter's the key,
In aquatic shadows, where we all long to be.

Anemones sway to this dreamy refrain,
In a world full of giggles, all worry is vain.
So dive into dreams, where humor abounds,
In the depths of the ocean, joy always sounds!

Tales from the Twilight Waters

In twilight's glow the fish all dance,
With fins and tails they take a chance.
A turtle sneezes, bubbles fly,
As seaweed giggles, oh my, oh my!

A crab with swagger walks the sand,
He's got a rockstar's band to command.
"Don't pinch me!" yells a passing shrimp,
As clams just chuckle, they can't help the imp!

Starfish tell tales of superhero spree,
While octopuses juggle cups of tea.
The anemones bob with sly delight,
As shells conspire to dance all night!

In the twilight waves, what a sight to see,
All creatures laughing, wild and free.
With every ripple, the stories grow,
In the sea's vast hall, the fun will flow!

Murmurings of the Blue Wilderness

Beneath the waves, a dolphin grins,
He's set to play some wacky spins.
"Watch me leap!" with a pipefish cheer,
While jellyfish float, they seem sincere.

A grouchy old fish with glasses on,
Complains about the kids' sweet song.
"Back in my day, we swam real cool!"
But bubbles burst; he's just a fool!

An urchin rolls his prickly ball,
"Come play with me" he calls to all.
But who would dare? They know the game,
A prickly friend is not the same!

Tides bring whispers of fits and quirks,
As sea cucumbers do silly jerks.
With every splash, a laugh erupts,
In the blue wilderness, joy corrupts!

Whispers Beneath the Waves

In shadows deep where sea dreams swirl,
An octopus twirls in a rainbow whirl.
With eight wiggly arms, he paints the sea,
Every stroke giggles, oh so free!

Clams play poker, it's quite a sight,
Their pearls all glimmer in the faint twilight.
A sneaky shrimp deals out the cards,
As fish trade secrets, oh what regards!

Sea horses boast of their latest fame,
"My bubble is bigger!" they play the game.
With a mermaid's laugh, they twirl about,
While anemones wish they'd just go out!

Beneath the waves, mischief reigns,
With every splash, joy breaks the chains.
A world alive with funny tales,
In ocean's heart, where laughter prevails!

Guardian of the Coral

A lionfish boasts with colors bright,
"I guard the coral, what a sight!"
But every time the clownfish tease,
His sharp little fins just love to freeze!

Sea turtles chuckle at all the fuss,
While shrimps complain, "Hey, it's not us!"
"Let's dance!" they cry in a bubbly tune,
Under the watch of the glowing moon.

A sleepy old puffer snores away,
As corals plan a salsa ballet.
"Let's show him how we can shake and sway!"
While starfish hum tunes from yesterday!

In coral gardens, laughter blooms,
Within the waves, the silliness looms.
A world of joy, colored and grand,
Where every critter has a funny plan!

Flickers of Life in Still Waters

Bubbles rise, fishy jokes made,
Coral giggles in the shade.
Dancing algae, a wobbly show,
Even the sea cucumbers glow!

Crabs wear glasses, looking smart,
Smirking shells, they play their part.
Octopus with eight left feet,
Stumbles on its way to eat!

Starfish collecting laugh-out-louds,
Floating grace beneath the clouds.
Lobster's tickles, a ticklish treat,
Ocean's laughter, oh so sweet!

With silly pals in shades of blue,
Underwater pranks, who knew?
As bubbles burst with giggles around,
Joyful waves are all around!

Beneath the Surface: Untold Stories

Clams gossip with a shellfish pride,
Fish in wigs take a wild ride.
Tales of dolphins' karaoke nights,
A splash of laughs and silly sights!

Turtles racing, slow but keen,
Whale songs echo, goofy and mean.
Seahorses in bow ties, so refined,
Jellyfish jiving, one of a kind!

Anemones tease with tickly arms,
While stingrays dance with pretty charms.
Eels pulling faces, oh what a sight,
Underwater giggles make it bright!

Every corner holds a tale,
In this watery fairytale.
With surprises lurking everywhere,
Deep sea laughs hang in the air!

The Quiet Sentinels of the Deep

Sponges soaking up the fun,
Nudibranchs dance, no need to run.
Flounders flopping, trying to hide,
But their funny faces can't be denied!

A crab spins tales with a sideways glance,
While sea urchins join in the dance.
Pufferfish puff with laughter loud,
Thoughts of being a spiky cloud!

In starry nights beneath the waves,
Laughs erupt from hidden caves.
Fishes trade jokes on coral reefs,
Where laughter lives, no room for griefs!

With a splash and a giggle, all are near,
Ocean's camaraderie, so sincere.
In waters blue and layers deep,
Silent friends, secrets they keep!

Silent Vigil Amongst the Currents

Among the waves, a giggle lurks,
Seashells whispering to the murks.
With flapping fins and silly spins,
Ocean's humor always wins!

Beneath the currents, pranks arise,
Witty fish with clever ties.
Prawns in tuxedos, oh so grand,
While jellyfish play in bands!

Turbulent tides, a laugh parade,
Bubble-blowing clowns in the shade.
Each twist and turn a wiggly joke,
Happiness bursts from every poke!

As coral reefs play host to cheer,
Marine comedians draw us near.
In watery depths where silliness thrives,
The joy of the sea forever derives!

The Watchful Eye of the Sea

In the depths where fish do prance,
A clam observes the ocean dance.
It giggles as a seahorse struts,
While peeling off its ancient nuts.

A hermit crab with fancy shell,
Got caught in seaweed, oh what a smell!
An octopus tries to juggle rocks,
But ends up tangled in his own socks.

A blenny jokes with a fish so bright,
"You shine too much; dim your light!"
They laugh while bubbles float above,
In a world where silliness reigns with love.

And as the waves whisper and chime,
The sea creatures giggle, it's party time!
In this underwater world of glee,
Watch closely — you might just find me!

Stillness of the Coral Kingdom

Corals sway with a gentle hum,
While fish parade in colors, oh so dumb.
A turtle winks, says, "Life's a show!"
Then trips on a weed, quite the low blow.

The starfish scolds a lazy snail,
"Get up! Move or you'll miss the mail!"
They gossip loudly, the crabs tune in,
Betting on which one will win the fin.

Anemones sway like they're in a trance,
Inviting clownfish for a dance.
Fish serve tacos to the seaweed crowd,
While dolphins cheer, they're feeling proud.

Stillness reigns, but laughter's loud,
In this vibrant, underwater crowd.
With every ripple, joy takes flight,
In the coral kingdom, all is bright!

Sentinels of the Underwater Realm

Guardians stare with their eyes aglow,
Watching fish in their crazy show.
A grouper grins, "Did you see that dive?"
A wrasse quips, "Looks more like a jive!"

Squids making ink clouds like it's art,
While eels play hide and seek, so smart.
A clam claps shells, setting the beat,
As seahorses twirl on their little feet.

The anglerfish lights up with pride,
"Who's the brightest of us, let's decide!"
But his glow flickers and loses spark,
"Oh never mind, it's just too dark."

Though sentinels keep their watchful aim,
Each funny blunder might stake a claim.
In this gentle world where laughter blooms,
Every coral holds secrets, maybe even cartoons!

Fables from the Deep Abyss

Beneath the waves where tales run wild,
A fish claims fame, looks quite beguiled.
"I swam so fast, no one could see!"
But a whale laughed, "I'm near infinity!"

Anemones tell tales of sneaky crabs,
"They pinch and run like little blabs!"
A dolphin shared tales from far-off shores,
While a clownfish acted like it was his chores.

Sea turtles share wisdom, oh so sly,
"Don't rush your swim, just enjoy the spy!"
A lesson lost on the darting fish,
Who raced to catch the jelly's swish.

Fables of laughter travel through time,
In the deep abyss where humor climbs.
With every ripple and splashing cheer,
Ocean's funny stories we hold so dear!

Vigil of the Marine Guardian

A crab with a beret, standing so proud,
Declares to the fish, "I'll say it out loud!"
"You think you can swim? You think you can dart?"
But the seaweed just giggles, it knows he's a fart.

A starfish on duty, with a badge made of kelp,
Keeps watch over clams, while they grumble and yelp.
"Hey, stop that tickling!" the mollusks all bid,
But who listens to starfish? Not any, they hid.

A dolphin named Sally, so sleek and so spry,
Jumps over the waves, to say her goodbye.
"I'll go catch a wave, watch my flip and my spin!"
But the wave just replies, "You'll just fall right back in!"

While octopuses dance in a kelp ballet,
They twirl and they twist, in a quirky display.
But their moves are so silly, the fish start to snicker,
As they launch into motions that pop like a ticker.

Chronicles of the Ocean Floor

A turtle took a selfie, with a shrimp on its lap,
"Say cheese, little buddy!" pretending to clap.
But the crab rolled its eyes, with a flick of a claw,
"Who needs all that nonsense? Just look at my jaw!"

The fish all gathered round, to hear stories so grand,
Of mermaids and shipwrecks, and cola on sand.
But the tales turned out boring, just bubbles and foam,
"Next time, bring a sea whale, he'll make it a poem!"

Anemones giggled, as the clownfish swam by,
With colors so bright, they could blind any eye.
But one fish got jealous, the grumpy old bass,
"Hey, you think you're so slick? Just wait till you pass!"

The ocean told secrets of quirky old lore,
Where eels would tell jokes and mermaids would snore.
And as tides came and went, the giggles would soar,
For laughter's the treasure deep down on the floor.

Silence Amongst the Anemones

In the sea of the quiet, where tickles abound,
The sea cucumbers gossip, from below to the ground.
"Did you hear about Sammy?" they whisper with glee,
"He tried to do backflips, forgot he was me!"

The clownfish got caught, in a garden so bright,
With anemones waving, all soft in the light.
"Hey buddy, just chill! You're all colorful flair!"
But Sammy end up stuck, in a rather bad hair!

A hermit crab strutted, in a shell made of gold,
"Look at me sparkle!" he cried, brave and bold.
But the seaweed just chuckled, as the currents did sway,
"You think you're so fancy, but dude, you're just gray!"

As bubbles erupted, and laughter took flight,
All the critters joined in, under moon's silver light.
For the ocean kept secrets, but laughter's the key,
To tickle the currents, set all thoughts free.

Beneath the Crystal Waters

A porpoise named Pete, danced loops in the sea,
"Look at me, everyone! Just as cool as can be!"
But a fish with a grin said, "You call that a twist?
I once spun like a blender, and you couldn't resist!"

Wandering seahorses, with their tails in a tangle,
Thought they were cute, but their friends had to wrangle.
"Hey! You're all knotted! It's a sight to behold!"
But they just kept swaying, not caring if bold.

An octopus chef, cooked pasta with flair,
"Who wants my great sauce? It's made with some air!"
But the fish all just laughed and then quickly dispersed,
"Who eats air-flavored pasta? You're clearly cursed!"

Within sparkling waves, the laughter ran deep,
As crabs cracked their jokes, while the sea turtles sleep.
Beneath all the currents, the joy was a treasure,
In this world full of giggles, where life is a pleasure.

Beneath the Ocean's Mask

Bubbles rise with giggling fish,
They dance and twirl, oh, what a swish.
A crab in shades, quite out of place,
He snaps his claws with comic grace.

A turtle wears a bubble hat,
He thinks he's cool, imagine that!
Dolphins in a conga line,
Splashing on like mermaid wine.

A starfish plays the ukulele,
Sings to a school of fish all day.
The octopus does funky moves,
While seaweed sways, the party grooves.

The clams all clap, they love the sound,
In this wild world where laughs abound.
Life beneath, with quirks galore,
Wonders found on the ocean floor.

Tales of the Forgotten Sea

A pirate fish with gold teeth grins,
He tells tales of where treasure bins,
A very lost, flamboyant shark,
Whispers rumors in the dark.

Jellyfish float with wobbly flair,
Pretend they're dancers in mid-air.
Seahorses giggle, do the twist,
While starry snails take a slow tryst.

In the depths, a clam holds court,
With seated fish, they laugh and snort.
A rogue wave joins the gossip tale,
Tales of mishaps that went stale.

Old sunken ships in humorous plight,
Gather round for a joke at night.
The vast blue, with comical glee,
Hides wild stories 'neath the sea.

Registers of the Blue Silence

In the stillness, a grouper slides,
With goofy wiggles, he decides.
A hermit crab behind a shell,
Is plotting pranks, oh what the hell!

Squids in suits play poker tight,
Ink-spilled cards make quite a sight.
With every draw, a laugh erupts,
As a clam 'folds'—oh, what's corrupt!

The seafloor holds comedic weight,
Fish tell tales of a bad date.
Nemo's in search of love so grand,
But always chooses the wrong sand.

Anemones wave, sharing their glee,
In the laughter of all that's free.
What secrets lie in waters deep,
With jokes that never let us sleep?

Beneath the Surface: Untold Stories

A curious dolphin takes a peek,
At sea cucumbers, so unique.
They grunt and groan with every sway,
Chasing each other in a play.

A tiny shrimp wears shades of pink,
Claims he's too cool, don't you think?
While the blowfish puffs with a grin,
Inviting all for a silly spin.

The angler fish tells a bright joke,
Lights up the room, oh what a bloke!
The puffer fish, not so bright,
Floats by, bloated from a fright.

With barnacles in a dance so wild,
And a snail who's crammed and simply smiled.
Submerged in laughter, a sea of cheer,
Beneath the waves, joy's always near.

Remnants of Ancient Reefs

Old corals boast of tales, quite grand,
With fish that dance and grains of sand.
They gossip with a wink and a wave,
Of sunken treasures and the daring brave.

Anemones chuckle at passing debris,
While turtles race by, oh so carefree.
Clownfish joke as they flip and dive,
In a world where the silly and clever thrive.

The sponges soak up the juicy dirt,
While shrimp crack jokes, you can hear their mirth.
This ancient realm, with laughter it's filled,
In underwater antics, never quite stilled.

They're planning a party, a grand ocean shindig,
With all sorts of sea life, it's bound to be big.
So if you dive down, be ready for cheer,
At the remnants of reefs where fun's always near.

Tales of the Current Watcher

A starfish lounges, claiming the floor,
As seahorses gossip, boasting galore.
The octopus winks, giving a sly grin,
While clams keep secrets tucked safely within.

The barnacles sing their crusty old song,
While jellyfish sway, oh so gracefully long.
Who knew the sea could be such a hoot?
With each current twist, it's hard to stay mute.

Fish don bow ties for fancy affairs,
As sea cucumbers flaunt their new wares.
The currents collude to spread all the news,
In this underwater realm, there's always good views.

So tune in, my friend, to the whispers below,
Where bubbles and giggles in harmony flow.
The current watcher's tales will surely amuse,
In a sea of antics, you've nothing to lose.

Underwater Chronicles

Bubbles rise up, as laughter takes flight,
In caverns of coral, what a dazzling sight!
The sea urchins wear hats, quite ridiculous,
While minnows assert they're quite meticulous.

Eels tell stories that twist and turn,
With every small flick, there's lessons to learn.
The clam's thick shell hides a smirk underneath,
As it chuckles aloud, oh what a deceit!

They gather in circles, exchanging wise cracks,
While a stealthy old crab expertly tracks.
A dolphin pops in with a joke or two,
Bringing forth giggles like morning dew.

These chronicles remind us, with humor and cheer,
That life in the ocean is bright and sincere.
Underwater laughter, oh what a thrill,
In shoals and in sways, it's a joyous drill!

Silent Shadows of the Ocean

In shadows, they plot, the fish all conspire,
To throw a big bash that no one will tire.
The seaweed stands by, all a-twirling with style,
While playful dolphins show off their best smile.

The stingrays glide in, looking quite sly,
Throwing high-fives as they flit by.
Anemones tease with their tickly embrace,
While octopuses juggle at a fevered pace.

In the stillness, the humor runs rife,
Between a clam's shivering and sea snail's strife.
Mollusks trade quips in a whispering tone,
In silent shadows, true laughter is sown.

So wonder not why the ocean's so bright,
Through shadows and secrets, there's always delight.
For in every wave, there's a pinch of jest,
Silent shadows hold joy, and it's always the best.

The Beneath Beneath

Under waves where fish do dance,
A crab wears shoes and takes his chance.
Jellyfish float, looking quite grand,
While seaweed sways, a band on the sand.

Starfish argue who wore the crown,
While octopuses swirl, they don't frown.
A clam rolls dice, it's quite the game,
Each twist of fate is never the same.

A dolphin giggles at a lost shoe,
While a turtle dreams of flying, it's true.
Dolphins in chairs sipping seaweed tea,
Are planning a showdown with the BBQ sea.

And when the tide pulls back in haste,
Sandy sneakers cause a big mess with taste.
With a wink and a wave to the sun above,
They laugh at the chaos, it's all out of love.

Reflections of the Deep Blue

Bubble bursts in a watery scene,
Sea cows float by, looking quite keen.
Mermaids gossip, wearing great hats,
While turtles pause to share silly chats.

A fish with a bow tie struts by,
He's heading to dinner, oh my, oh my!
Clams hold a feast with pearls on display,
Eels provide music, dancing away.

Where sea urchins trade stocks and trends,
Anemones sell cotton candy to friends.
The light from above creates shadows that box,
While crabs play the piano with their hard-shelled socks.

As seahorses swing in a jolly parade,
Each one moves with a bold charade.
In this world under, fun's always near,
With laughter and giggles to fill every sphere.

Ocean's Quiet Conspirator

In the depths where secrets swim far,
A fish with a mustache dreams of a car.
Seashells whisper tales from the sand,
While crabs plot a show – oh, isn't life grand?

A playful otter steals a net,
Dreaming of sushi, a tasty duet.
Grouper chefs serve up laughs with their flair,
As sunbeams dance without any care.

A troupe of small fish lines up to dance,
While seagulls bet if crabs have a chance.
Coral reefs hold court for a rousing debate,
About who is the best at doing the gait.

When sharks show up with party hats,
The undersea revelers, oh how they chat!
Laughter bubbles up in the warm, salty tide,
As the ocean hums secrets with great pride.

The Unseen Keeper of the Tide

In a world where shadows dance on the floor,
A lobster counts stars, despite being a chore.
Seashell commanders plot with great zeal,
While fish in disguises shout, 'What a deal!'

A whale plays tag, oh what a sight,
While sea cucumbers cheer with delight.
An undersea party, bright and bizarre,
Where sea urchins argue who's the best star.

The laughter echoes through waves and froth,
As sea horses play jumper, a flip and a troth.
A turtle can't dance but tries all the same,
Proclaiming to all he's invented a game.

With a flick of a fin, and a splash of dismay,
They spin their tales in the glimmering spray.
Each wave brings a chuckle, each tide brings a grin,
Together they celebrate, let the jokes begin!

Underwater Chronicles of Resilience

A fish in a tie, looks quite debonair,
He schools with his friends, without a single care.
They gossip 'bout currents, and the clumsy crab,
Who thought he could dance, but just made us blab.

The seahorse plays poker, very sly and spry,
With a wink and a flip, the stakes get quite high.
The octopus deals cards from a jellyfish hat,
While a clam munches chips, now how 'bout that?

A clam with a dream, to sing like a bard,
But his voice, oh so flat, is simply too hard.
The fish just swim by, trying not to snicker,
As the clam belts a tune, it gets louder and thicker.

A dolphin jokes loudly, splashes all around,
While the coral just laughs at the silliness found.
Under waves full of whimsy, they share tales of strife,
In the curious depths, they're just full of life.

The Pulse of the Sea's Silence

A turtle who's slow, yet thinks he's a jet,
Swims circles around, taking bets on his stamina yet.
He hums to the currents, a tune quite bizarre,
While a sponge on the side shouts, "Dude, you're a star!"

A crab with a monocle poses with flair,
Declares, "I'm the ruler of this aquatic lair!"
But every time he tries to take charge of the crowd,
He stumbles on seaweed, and the fish laugh out loud.

The pufferfish puffs, thinking he's tough,
But all that he's got is just too much fluff.
He floats like a balloon, but it's all in good fun,
While the angelfish tease, "Come on, you're done!"

In this underwater world, shenanigans thrive,
With sea creatures laughing, just happy to dive.
A playful ballet, where silence gets cheered,
Beneath the blue waves, their joy never veered.

Guardians of Forgotten Depths

A grumpy old grouper, with tales of the past,
Tells stories of treasures, that his buddies amassed.
But when the sun's shining, and currents run free,
They leave him to mutter his "glory" at sea.

An eel with a wink, slithers by with a grin,
Brags about finding some pearls wrapped in tin.
The fish shake their heads, as he shares his tall tales,
Of encounters with sharks and mermaids with scales.

A pair of sea lions, too silly for grace,
Compete for a throne, with a clam for a base.
One leaps through the air, with an over-the-top twist,
While the other just tumbles, "This isn't my list!"

As laughter erupts, the storylines blend,
With every old tale, new laughs they transcend.
Under waves of their world, so carefree and bright,
They cherish their time, in the warm ocean light.

Beneath the Calm

A starfish surveys as the bubbles take flight,
While a crab tells a joke, that just feels so right.
"Why did the fish blush?" he starts with a grin,
"Cause he saw the ocean's bottom, and that's where we've been!"

Anemones sway, in rhythm to the tunes,
As the clownfish prance, under glow of the moons.
They twirl and they twist with flair so sublime,
Causing a ruckus, while dancing through time.

A seahorse rides waves, like a surfer elite,
While jellyfish drift, dancing from beat to beat.
"Join the parade!" calls the flounder, on cue,
"Stick with me, friends, and we'll color the blue!"

Beneath all the calm, silliness unfolds,
With laughter and joy, as the ocean upholds.
Their antics and pranks, in the most whimsical way,
Create a bright world, where they frolic and play.

Voices Resound

A whale told a tale, oh so grand and profound,
His friends rolled their eyes, heard it twice from the sound.
Yet with every deep note, like a curious echo,
They giggled along, for his stories were special.

A squid with a quirk, dreams of being a star,
And inks out his plans for his future bazaar.
But every time he spreads his silken delight,
He ends with a splash, giving everyone fright!

A hermit crab fancies a snazzy new shell,
While the other seashells can't help but compel.
"Pick me!" they all shout, as he scuttles about,
With laughter that travels, you can hear the shout.

As waves go to whisper, the fun still resounds,
In currents of joy, where friendship abounds.
Together they flourish, with humor and cheer,
In depths of the ocean, where all creatures appear.

The Ocean's Hidden Eyes

Beneath the waves, they glance and peep,
A crab in shades, keeping secrets deep.
The fish wear smiles, so sly and bright,
They giggle and dance, under moonlight.

Octopus grins, with eight arms spread,
Playing hide and seek, in seaweed bed.
Starfish are cheering, stuck to the sand,
Rooting for fish, in this playful band.

A dolphin flips, caught in a light,
Making fish fall, in an acrobatic flight.
The sea turtles chuckle, slow and grand,
As bubbles rise up, they form a band.

In a world of splash, joy spills out,
Where laughter flows, there's always a shout.
Underwater antics, a genuine feast,
In the laughter of depths, not the least!

Secrets Lurking in Turquoise Depths

Turtles discuss, over algae toast,
About the fish, who boast and boast.
One with a crown, says he's the king,
While others swim fast, not giving a fling.

Seahorses giggle, in neon hues,
Chasing the bubbles like colorful blues.
They whisper of tales from long ago,
When crabs wore hats, and danced in a row.

Anemones sway, a party in sway,
Catch the clown fish, laughing away.
Lobsters in tuxes, all dressed up neat,
Join in the fun, moving their feet.

In a play of shades, the sea's alive,
Where humor swims easily and thrives.
A jester in currents, with jokes to share,
In depths of laughter, life's never bare!

Murmurs from the Marine Abyss

Whale songs echo, a deep bass line,
While squids are sketching, a dance so fine.
Gregarious groupers gossip with grace,
Secretly planning the clams' next race.

Eels start to wiggle, with a giggly spurt,
While shrimps crack jokes, in coral shirt.
They chime in chorus, with splashes of cheer,
Creating a hullabaloo, down in the sphere.

Puffer fish puff, they say it's a jest,
Making themselves look big is their quest.
Bubbles burst outward, a cacophonous cheer,
In every fun splash, no room for fear!

In the silent blue, where jokes run deep,
The laughter unfurls, in bubbles that leap.
A comedy club, in currents so vast,
In the ocean's embrace, all worries are cast!

Chronicles of the Silent Sea

A clam tells stories, in muted tones,
While sea urchins roll, over ancient bones.
The jellyfish waltz, with grace in the night,
Twinkling like stars, a whimsical sight.

Coral reefs whisper, laughs trapped in light,
As plankton dance by, in a frolicsome flight.
The clownfish prance, round anemone beds,
Playful and sprightly, filling the heads.

Urchins are jesters, on rocky old seats,
Filling the sea with their humorous beats.
An orchestra plays, in waves of delight,
As fish hold hands, in a twinkling fright.

Beneath the wave's crest, tales bloom and flow,
In a heartfelt chorus, where funny things grow.
An epic of glee, in the ocean they find,
A laugh-filled journey, beautifully entwined!

www.ingramcontent.com/pod-product-compliance
Lightning Source LLC
Chambersburg PA
CBHW060142230426
43661CB00003B/534